DE SEPTEM SECUNDEIS

DE SEPTEM SECUNDEIS

JOHN TRITEMIUS

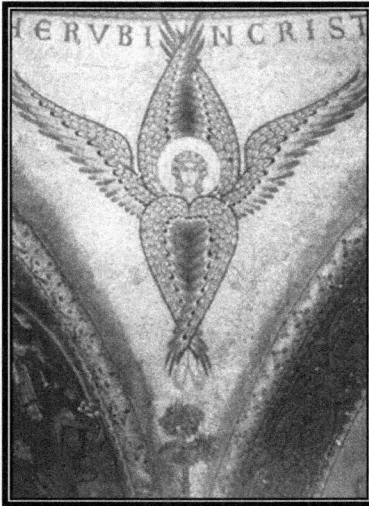

ON THE SEVEN SECONDARY CAUSES OF THE HEAVENLY
INTELLIGENCES, GOVERNING THE ORBS UNDER GOD.

Translated 1647, by William Lilly

DEDICATION:

to the Emperor Maximilian

Renowned Caesar, it is the opinion of very many of the Ancients, that this inferious World by ordination of the first *Intellect* (which is God) is directed and ordered by *Secundarian Intelligences,* to which opinion *Conciliator Medicorum* assents, saying, that from the Original or first beginning of heaven and earth, there were seven spirits appointed as Presidents to the seven planets.

Of which number every one of those rules the world 354 years, and four months in order.

To this Position, many, and they most learned men, have afforded their consent; which opinion of theirs *myself* not affirming, but delivering, do make manifest to your most sacred Majesty.

6

DE SEPTEM SECUNDEIS

The first Angel or Spirit of *Saturn* is called *Orifiel*, to whom God committed the government of the World from the beginning of its Creation; who began his government the 15th day of the month of *March*, in the first year of the World, and it endured 354 years and 4 months.

Orifiel notwithstanding is a name appertaining to his Office, not his Nature. Attributed to the Spirit in regard of his action, under his dominion men were rude, and cohabited together in desert and uncouth places, living after the manner of Beasts. This does not need any manner of proof from me, since its so manifest out of the Text of Genesis.

The second Governor of the World is *Anael* the Spirit of *Venus*, who after *Orifiel* began to rule according to the influence of this Planet, in the year of the world 354. the fourth month, that is, the 24 day of the month of *June*, and he ruled the world 354 years, and 4 months, until the year from the Creation of the world

708, as it would appear to any that shall Calculate the Age thereof.

Under the Regiment of this Angel, men began to be more Civilized, built Houses, erected Cities, discovered the Manufacturing Arts: the Art of Weaving, Spinning, and Cloathing, and many such like as these, and indulged themselves plentifully with the pleasures of the flesh, took unto themselves fair women for their wives, neglected God, Receded in many things from their natural simplicity; they discovered Sports, and Songs, sang to the Harp, and did excogitate whatsoever did belong to the worship and purpose of *Venus*. And this wantonness of life by mankind continued until the flood, receiving the Arguments of its pravity ever since.

Zachariel the Angel of *Jupiter,* began to govern the world in the year of the Creation of Heaven and Earth 708 the eighth month, that is, the 25 day of the month of *October,* and he regulated the World 354 years, 4 months, until the year of the worlds Creation 1063, inclusively. Under whose moderation, men first of all began to usurp Dominion over one another, to exercise Hunting, to make Tents, to adorn their bodies with several garments: and there arose a great Division between good and evil men; the Pious invoking God, such as *Enoch,* whom the Lord translated to Heaven' the wicked running after the snares and pleasant allurements of the Flesh.

Men also under the Dominion of this *Zachariel* began to live more civilly, to undergo the Laws and Commands of their Elders, and were reclaimed from their former fierceness. Under his rule *Adam* the first man died, leaving to all posterity an assured Testimony, that it was certain that we all must die, eventually.

Various Arts and Inventions of men did about this time first appear and manifest themselves, as Historians have more clearly expressed.

The fourth Rector of the World was *Raphael,* the Spirit of *Mercury* which began in the year of the Creation of Heaven and Earth 1063 the 24th day of *February,* and he reigned 354 years 4 months, and his Government continued until the year of the World 1417 and fourth month. In these times writing was first discovered, and letters resembling Trees and Plants, which notwithstanding afterwards and in process of time, received a more graceful shape, and the Nations varied or changed the Face of their Characters according to their own fancy. The use of Musical Instruments, under the time and rule of *Raphael,* began to be multiplied, and Commerce or Exchange between men was now first invented: A presumptuous, rude and simple Audacity in these times begot Navigation or the manner of Sailing from one place to another, and many such like things in one kinde or other, etc.

The fifth *Gubernator* of the World was *Samuel* the Angel of *Mars,* who began the 26 day of the month of *June* in the year of the World 1417, and swayed the rule of this World 354 years 4 months, until the year of the World 1771 and the eighth month, under whose Empire and Government men imitated the nature of *Mars,* also under the Dominion of this Angel, the Universal deluge of waters happened *Anno Mundi* 1656, as evidently it appears by History out of *Genesis*. And its to be observed, what the ancient Philosophers have delivered, that so oft as *Samuel* the Angel of *Mars* is ruler of the World, so often there arises notable alterations of Monarchy. Religions and sects vary, Laws are changed, Principalities and Kingdoms are transferred to Strangers, which we may easily find out in order by the perusal of Histories.

Notwithstanding *Samuel* does not immediately, in the very beginning or entrance of his Dominion, manifest the disposition of his behaviour or custom: but when he has exceeded the middle time of his *Gubernation,* which very thing is likewise to be understood concerning the Angels of the other Planets, (as it may be manifested from Histories) all which send down their influence according to the Proprieties of the natures of their Stars, and operate upon the inferior bodies of this World.

The sixth Governor of the World is *Gabriel* the Angel of the Moon, who began after *Samuel* the Angel of *Mars* had finished his course upon the 28 day of the month of *October* in the year of the World 1771 and eighth month: and he ordered the affairs of the World 354 years and 4 months, until the year of the World 2126. Again in these times men were multiplying, and built many Cities, and we must note: that the Hebrews affirm that the General deluge, was *Anno Mundi 1656* - under the moderation of *Mars*: But the Septuagint interpreters, *Isidorus* and *Beda* confirm the Deluge to be in the year of the World 2242 under the Regiment of Gabriel, the Angel of the Moon, which seems to me by Multiplication to be consistent with the truth, but to express my further conception hereof, is not the work of this present discourse.

Michael the Angel of the Sun was the 7th Ruler of the World, who began the 24th of *February*, in the year of the World according to common computation 2126, and he governed the world 354 years and four months, until the year of the age of the world 2480 and four months.

Under the Dominion of the Angel of the Sun even as Histories consent with truth, Kings began first to be amongst Mortal men, of whom *Nimrod* was the first, that with an ambitious desire of Sovereignty, did Tyrannize over his Companions.

The worship of several Gods by the foolishness of men, was now instituted, and they began to adore their petty Princes as Gods.

Sundry Arts also about this time were invented by men; to wit, the Mathematics, Astronomy, Magic, and that worship, which formerly was attributed to the one and only God, began now to be given to diverse Creatures: the knowledge of the true God, by little and little, through the superstition of men, became forgotten.

About these times Architecture was discovered, and men began to use more policy both in their civil institutions, and manners, or customs of living.

From this time, the eighth time in order, again *Orifiel* the Angel of *Saturn* began to govern the World on the

26th day of the month of *June,* in the year from the beginning of the world 2480 and the fourth month; and he continued his government of the world this second return, 354 years and four months, until the year of the world 2834. and eight months. Under the regulation of this Angel, the Nations were multiplied, and the earth was divided into Regions; many Kingdoms were instituted; the Towel of *Babel* was built, the confusion of Tongues then fell out, men were dispersed into every part of the earth, and men began to Till, and Manure the earth more acurately, to ordain Fields, sow Corn, plant Vineyards, to dig up Trees, and to provide with greater diligence, what ever was more convenient for their food, and rainment.

From that time forward, first of all, amongst men, the discerning of Nobility begun to be noticed; which was, when men in their manner of living, and in wisdom excelled the rest of men, undertaking Trophies of glory from the great ones of the earth, as rewards for their merits: From this time, first of all, the whole world began to come into the knowledge of men, while everywhere the Nations were being multiplied, many Kingdoms arose, and various differences of tongues followed.

The ninth time in order and course, *Anael,* the Angel of *Venus* began again to sway the world the 29th day of *October* in the year of the Creation of Heaven and earth 2834 and the 8th month: and he presided 354 years and four months, until the year of the world 3189.

In these times men forgetting the true God, began to honour the dead, and to worship their Statues for God, the Error which infected the World for more than two thousand years. Men now devised curious and costly Ornaments, for better trimming, and adorning their bodies, found out diverse kindes of Musical Instruments. Again, men prosecuted too much the lust and pleasures of the flesh, instituting, and dedicating Statues and Temples to their Gods. Witchcraft, and Incantations in these times were first excogitated by *Zoroaster* King of the *Bactrians* (and diverse others as well as he) whom *Ninus* King of *Assyria* overcame in War.

In order the tenth time *Zachariel* the Angel of *Jupiter*, again began to rule the world the last day of *February*, in the year of the building, or framing the heaven and earth, 3189. And he moderated according to his custom and manner 354 years, and four months, until the year of the world 3543 and four months.

These were joyful times, and might truly be called golden, wherein there was plenty of all manner of useful things, which much conducive for the increase of mankind, giving thereby exceeding beauty and adornment to the things of this World.

In like manner about this time, God gave to *Abraham* the *Law* of *Circumcision*; and first of all promised the *Redemption* of *Mankind* by the *Incarnation* of his only begotten Son.

Under the Government of this Angel, the Patriarchs, the first *Founders* of *Justice*, were famous, and the righteous were divided from the ungodly, by their own proper indeavor and consent.

13

About these times in *Arcadia*, *Jupiter* grew famous, who was styled also *Lisania*, the Son of Heaven and God, a King, who first of all gave Laws to the Arcadians, made them very civil in their manners and behaviour, taught them the worship of God, erected them Temples, instituted Priests, procured many advantagious benefits for mankind, for which his so great benefits, he was by them termed *Jupiter*, and after his death was accounted for as a *Deity* or a God.

He had his Original from the sons of *Heber*, *viz. Gerar*, as ancient Histories do record to posterity.

Prometheus also the son of *Atlas* is reported under the Government of this Angel to have made Men; only, because of their rudeness and ignorance, he made them wise and knowing, humane, courteous, accomplished in learning and manners: he made Images by Art to move of themselves.

He first found out the use of the Ring, Scepter, Diadem, and all kingly ornaments.

In or about these times other jovial men excelled; *men* most wise, and *women* also, who by their own understanding delivered many profitable inventions to mankind; who being dead, for the greatness of their wisdom, were reputed as Gods: *viz. Photoneus*, who first of all instituted amongst the Greeks, Laws, and judgements, as also, *Sol, Minerva, Ceres, Serapis* amongst the *Aegyptians,* and very many besides.

In order the 11th time, *Raphael* the Angel of *Mercury* again undertook the ordering of the world the first day of the month of *July*, in the year of the world 3543 and the fourth month; he continued in his Commands 354 years, and four months, until the year of the Creation of heaven and earth 3897 and 8 months.

Verily in these times, as it evidently appears from the Histories of the Ancients, men more earnestly applied themselves to the study of wisdom, amongst whom the last learned and most eminent men, were *Mercurius, Bacchus, Omogyius, Isis, Inachus, Argus, Apollo, Cecrops*, and many more, who by their admirable inventions, both profited the world then, and in posterity since.

Several Superstitions also about these times, concerning the worship of their Idols were instituted by men.

Sorceries, Incantations, and Arts of framing Diabolical Images, were now in a marvelous manner increased, and whatsoever either of subtlety, or wit, that could possibly be attributed to the invention, or cunning of *Mercury* about these times, exceedingly increased.

Moses the wisest Commander of the Hebrews, expert in the knowledge of many things and Arts, a Worshipper of the one, only true God, deliverd the people of *Israel* from the slavery of the *Aegyptians*, and procured their liberty.

About this time *Janus* first of all reigned in *Italy*, after him *Saturnus*, who instructed his people to fat their grounds with soil or dung, and was accounted or esteemed for a God.

Near these times *Cadmus* found out the Greek Letters, or Characters, and *Carmentis*, the daughter of *Evander*, the Latin.

God Omnipotent, under the Government of this *Raphael*, the Angel of *Mercury*, delivered by the hands of *Moses*, to his people a Law in writing, which gave manifest testimony of our Saviour *Jesus Christ*, his future birth and nativity to be born in the flesh.

Here arose in the World a wonderful diversity of Religions: During these times, here flourished many *Sybills, Prophets, Diviners, Soothsayers*, or such as used inspection into the entrails of Beasts, *Magitians*, or *Wise-men, Poets*, as *Sybilla, Erythraea*, she of the Isle of *Delphos*, she whom we call the Phrygian, because she lived in *Phrygia* with the rest.

Again in order the twelfth time, *Samuel* the Angel of *Mars*, began to exercise his Dominion upon the world, the second day of the month of *October*, in the year of the world 3897 and the eighth month, and his time of ruling, was 354 years, and four months from then, until the year 4252 under whose Empire and rule, was that great and most famous Destruction of *Troy* in *Asia* the less: as also an admirable mutation, and alteration of *Monarchy*, and many Kingdoms together with new institutions, or moldings of many Cities, as *Paris, Monunce, Carthage, Naples*, and very many besides these.

Many new Kingdoms were newly erected, or now had their first beginning, as that of the *Lacedemonians, Corinthians, Hebrews,* and many others.

Here in these times all over the whole world, there were very great wars, and Battles of Kings and Nations, and several alterations of Empires.

The Venetians from this time, compute and reckon the original both of their people and City from the Trojans.

And its observable that very many other Nations, as well in *Europe* as in *Asia,* pretend to have taken their original from the Trojans, to whom I thought good to give so much credit, as they themselves were able to persuade me was truth, upon sufficient testimony and proof.

The Arguments they produce concerning their Nobility and Antiquity are frivolous, being desirous to magnify themselves openly, as if there were no People, or Nation in *Europe,* before the Destruction of *Troy,* or as if there had been no Pesant, or Clown amongst the Trojans.

Under the moderation also of this Planet, *Saul* was made first King of the Jews, after him *David,* whose son King *Salomon,* built in *Jerusalem* the Temple of the true God, the most famous and glorious of the whole world: from hence the Spirit of God illustrating, and enlightening his Prophets with a more ample illumination of his grace, they did not only foretel of the future incarnation of our Lord and Saviour, but also many other things, as holy Scriptures do testify, amongst whom were Nathan son of King *David, Gad, Asaph, Achias, Semeias, Asarias, Anan,* and many others.

Homer the Greek Poet, writer of *Troys* Destruction, *Dares, Phrygius, Dyctis Cretensis,* who were themselves at the razing, and sacking thereof, and have likewise described it, are supported to have been alive near about these times.

The thirteenth time in order, *Gabriel* the Spirit of the Moon, again undertook the ordering of this world the 30th day of *January* in the year from the beginning of the *Universe* 4252, and he presided in his Government 354 years, 4 months, until the year of the World 4606, and the fourth month.

In this time many Prophets were famous and excelled amongst the Jews, videlicet: *Helias, Heliseus, Micheas, Abdias,* with many others: There were many alterations of the Kingdom of the Jews: *Lycurgus* gave Laws and Ordinances to the *Lacedemonians, Capetus, Sylvius. Lyberius Sylvius, Romulus Sylvius, Procas Sylvius, Numitor,* Kings of *Italy* flourished, during the moderation of this spirit: more Kingdoms also had their Original or foundation under him, as those of the *Lydians, Medes, Macedonians, Spartans,* and others: the Monarchy of *Assyrians* under *Sardanapalus* now ended. And in like manner the Kingdom of the *Macedonians* was consumed, or worn out.

Sundry laws are imposed on men, the worship of the true God is neglected, and the Religion of false Gods is propagated too much: the City of Rome is built under the Dominion of this Spirit, in the year 1484, which year in order, was the 239 of the Angel *Gabriel*, the Kingdom of the *Sylvans* in *Italy* now ended, and that of *Rome* began in these times, *Thales, Chilon, Periander, Cleobulus, Bias, and Pittacus,* the seven wise men of Greece florished, and from thence Philosophers and Poets came into request. At *Rome, Romulus* the first founder of the City reigned 37 years being a Fratricide and a stirrer up of Sedition. After whom *Numa Pompilius* continued that Kingdom in peace for a full 42 years: he amplified the worship of the Gods, and lived in the time of *Hezekiah,* King of *Judea.* About the expiration of this Angel of the Moon his government: *Nebuchadonozor* King of *Babylon,* took *Jerusalem,* and destroyed *Zedechiah* the King and carryed away all the people Captive.

Jeremiah the Prophet was now famous, who fore-told this destruction, as also their future delivery from *Babylon.*

When *Gabriel* had finished his course, again *Michael,* Angel of the Sun, assumed the 14th government of the World, who began the first day of the month of *May,* in the year of the World, 4606 and the fourth month, and ruled the World according to his own order 354 years, until the year of the Worlds Creation, 4960 and the eighth month.

In the time of this Angels moderation *Evil Merodach* King of *Babylon,* restored both their Liberty and King to the people of the Jews, according to the direction of the Angel *Michael,* who as *Daniel* wrote, stood for the

Nation of the Jews, unto whom they were committed by God.

In these times, likewise, the Monarchy of the Kingdom of the Persians began, whose first King *Darius*: and the second *Cyrus* brought to nothing or utterly ruined, that most powerful Kingdom of *Babylon* in the days of *Balthazar*, (as *Daniel* and the Prophets had predicted.)

In these times *Sybilla Cumana* was much spoken of, and grew famous; who brought 9 books to *Tarquinius Priscus* the King to be bought for a certain price; in which were contained the reason, order, and succession of future Advisements, of the whole commonwealth of the Romans. But when the King refused to give her the price demanded, *Sybilla* (the King seeing it) burnt the three first books, demanding the same price for the other six; which when again he had denied to give her, she committed to be burnt three of those remaining, and would have done so by the rest; unless the King by persuasion and through the Councel of others, had not redeemed them from such consumption, giving the same price for the last three, for which he might have had the whole nine.

Moreover the Romans having abrogated Government by Kings constituted two Consuls to reign every year.

Phalaris the Tyrant in these times occupied *Sicilia: Magique* or natural Philosophy was also, in these times, highly esteemed amongst the Kings of *Persia*.

Pythagoras the Philosopher, and very many others, flourished amongst the *Greeks;* the Temple and City of *Jerusalem* was now rebuilt.

Esdras the Prophet repaired the books of *Moses,* burned by the *Chaldeans*; who were also called *Babylonians,* and committed them to memory for example. *Xerxes* King of the *Persians* brought his Army against the *Greeks,* but had no success therein. The City of *Rome* is taken, burned, and destroyed, by the *Gaules*; the Capitol only preserved by a Goose, stirring up the weary Champions. The *Athenians* had eminent wars in these times: *Socrates et Plato* Philosophers lived now.

The Romans lessened the power of their Consuls, instituted *Tribunes et Aedils,* and were also about these times involved in many calamities: *Alexander* the great after the expiration of the rule of *Michael,* reigned in *Macedonia,* destroyed the Monarchy of the *Persians* in *Darius*: conquered all *Asia,* and annexed it with part of *Europe* to his own Empire.

He lived 33 years, reigned 12 after whose death infinite wars and many mischiefs followed, and his Monarchy became divided amongst four.

Now amongst the Jews, first of all, they began to contend for the Priesthood: the Kingdom of *Syria* began.

After the Spirit of *Michael* had finished his course, then the 15th time in order, *Orifiel* the Angel of *Saturn,* the third time assumed the regulating of this World, during the last day of the month of *September*, in the year from the building of the *Universe*, 4960 and the eighth month: and he ruled in Chief 354 years, 4 months, until the year of the World 5315. Under whose moderation, the *Punick* war began between the *Romans* and *Carthaginians*: the City of *Rome* was almost wholly consumed by fire and water. The Brazen Molten Image called *Colossus*, in length one hundred and twenty six feet, fell down, being shaken by an earthquake. At, or near this time the City of *Rome* enjoyed peace one year after the *Punick* War: which Common-wealth had never been without War in 440 years before.

Jerusalem together with the Temple is burnt and destroyed by *Antiochus* and *Epiphanes*, the History of the *Machabees* and their Wars were now acted.

In these times *Carthage* 606 years after its first foundation is destroyed, and burned continually by the space of 17 whole days. In *Sicilia* seventy thousand slaves made a Conspiracy against their Masters.

Many *Prodigies* in these times were beheld in *Europe*; tame domestic cattle fled to the Woods, it rained blood, a fiery Ball shined, appeared, and glistered out of heaven with great noise and crackling. *Mithridates* King of *Pontus*, and *Armenia* held Wars with the *Romans* over 40 years. The Kingdom of the Jews is restored, which had interruption 575 years from the time of *Zedechia* until *Aristobalus*. The people also of *Germany* called the *Theutines*, invaded the *Romans* and after many fights are overcome and one hundred and threescore thousand of them slain, besides innumerable others of them, who slew themselves and familiars under *Cajus* and *Mantius* the Consuls: notwithstanding this, many of the *Romans* were before this cut off by them: after which time, Civill Wars did much shake the *Romane* Common-wealth, which endured full 40 years. Three *Suns* appeared and were seen in *Rome*, but not long ere they were reduced into one.

A very few years succeeding, *Julius Cajus Caesar* usurped the government of the *Romans*, which *Octavius Augustus* after him amplified, and joyned *Asia, Africk* and *Europe* into one Monarchy he reigned 36 years by whom, or whose means God gave peace to the whole World: In the year from the building of the City 751. and of *Caesar Octavius Augustus* 42. and in the 245 year and eighth month, the 25 of *December*, of the government of the aforesaid *Orifiel* the Angel of *Saturne*: Iesus Christ the Son of God is born in *Bethelem* of *Iudea*, of *Mary* the Virgin. Note, how faire and wonderfull the Ordination of Divine providence is; for the World at first was created under the rule of *Saturn* his Angel *Orifiel*: and mercifully redeemed, instaurated, and made new again under his third government; so that the great number and agreement of concurring Actions, may seem to administer no small beliefe to this manner of description, or setting forth, that this World is governed by the seaven Angels of the Planets: for in the first Gubernation of *Orifiel*, there was one only Monarchy of the whole World, under his second (as we mentioned before) it was divided amongst many.

Again, during his third, (as is manifest) it was reduced into one, although, if we consider or measure time aright, it is manifest also that in the second government of *Orifiel*, there was but one only Monarchy, when the Tower of *Babel* was built. From this time forward the Kingdom of the Jews was quite taken away, and the sacrifice of meat-offerings ceased, nor shall liberty be restored to the Jews before the third Revolution of the Angel *Michael*, and this shall be after the Nativity of Christ, in the year 1880, in the eighth month, videlecit In the year of the World 7170. and eight months. Many of the Jews in those times, and of the Gentiles also, shall embrace Christian Religion, most plain and simple men preaching the word of God, whom no human institution, but a divine spirit hath inspired. The World shall then be brought to its first innocency of its simplicity, the Angel of *Saturne Orifiel* governing the World every where.

Celestial things are mixed with earthly, many of the Christians, for that faith which they Preached, shall be slaughtered by the rulers of this World. About the ending of the Moderation of *Orifiel, Jerusalem* is destroyed by the *Romans*, and the *Jews* are dispersed into every Nation, there being massacred of them eleven hundred thousand, and four score thousand sold for slaves, the residue of them fled; and so the *Romans* wholly destroyed *Judea*.

After *Orifiel* had finished his government, *Anael* the Angel of *Venus*, the sixteenth in order, the third time reassumed his Regiment of the World: the last day of *January*, in the year of creating the Heaven and the Earth 5315, but from the year of the birth of Christ 109, and he regulated the affairs of the World 354 years and 4 months, until the years of the World 5669 and 4 months, but of the Nativity of our Savior Jesus Christ in the flesh 463. And it's remarkable, that almost during the whole rule of this *Anael* the Angel of *Venus*, the Church of Christians flourished in her persecutions, and prevailed; many thousands, of men being Butchered for the Faith of Christ. Moreover in these times, very many Heresies began to be broached in the Church, which were not extinguished, but only after some time, and with labour and the blood of good men.

Many men were eminent about these times in all manner of learning, and such as were learned and Eloquent Diviners, Astronomers, Physitians, Orators, Historiographers, and men of like quality, not only amongst the *Gentiles*, but *Christians*. At length the persecution of *Infidels* ceased, after that *Constantine Caesar* the great, had assumed the Christian faith, in the year of the World 5539, after the middle of the Government of the aforesaid *Anael* the Angel of *Venus*. Although those professing the Religion and faith of Iesus Christ in some measure were now and then disturbed and molested by the Ungodly; Yet notwithstanding the peace of the Church did remain free from molestation a long time.

From this time forward, Mankind which from the time of *Ninus* the King, for almost the space of two thousand and three hundred years, had most miserably gone astray about the worship of Idols, was now revoked mercifully to the knowledge of one only God.

Various Arts of Subtlety in these times were augmented, and had increase and reputation according to their convenience to the nature of *Venus*.

For the manners of men are changed with the time, and the inferior bodies are disposed according to the influence of the superiors.

The mind of man (verily) is free, and receives not the influence of the Stars, unless it does too much commaculate his affection, by inclining its self with the commerce which it has with the body. For the Angels who are the movers of the Orbs, neither destroy nor subvert any thing, which nature it self has constituted or framed.

A Comet of unwonted and unusual greatness preceded the death of *Constantine*.

The *Arrian* Heresie in many Countries disturbed the holy Church.

Toward the end of this Angels Government, in the time of *Julianus Caesar*, Crosses appeared in lines, and Crosses in the garments of men.

In *Asia* and *Palaestina* wars followed, Pestilences and Famine in those places where the Crosses appeared.

In these times also about the year of our Lord 360. the *Franks* or *Franconians* in *Germany* had their Originall; who afterwards wasting *Gallia*, gave the name unto it of *France*, having first overcome and conquered the people thereof. The description of *Francia* in greatness

26

is long and wide, or of great circuit, whose *Metropolis Moguntia* sometimes was; now truly and only *Herbipolis*.

The *Bavarians, Suevians*, the people of *Rhine, Saxons, Thuringers*, this day do occupy a great part of *France* in *Germany*, under jurisdiction of the *Papacy* in some places. Moreover in the 280 year of the Gubernation of this Angel *Anael*, the *Roman Empire* began to decline, while the City was taken and burned by the *Goths* the *Imperial* seat being first translated into *Greece* under *Constantine*, which was very mischievously done, and the only cause of the declining of that whole Monarchy: for near the determination of this Angel *Anael* his Regiment, there did arise *Radigifus, Alaricus, Atholfus*, Kings of the *Gothes*: Also after this *Genserick* of the *Vandals* and *Attilas* of the *Hunns* who running all over *Europe*, did most miserably tear the Empire assunder, as is evident in these Histories.

When *Anael* the Angel of *Venus* had finished his Regiment, then *Zachariel* the Spirit of *Jupiter* reassumed the Universal Government of this World the seventh time, the first day of *June*, in the year of the World 5669 and the fourth month, but in the year of our Lord and Saviour Jesus Christ 463 and four months; and governed in his turn 354 years and four months until the year of the World 6023 and the eighth month: but of our Lord God 817.
Many men in these times out of their affection to Christian Philosophy, took themselves to live in the Wilderness: many Prodigies appeared, Comets, Earthquakes, it rained blood.

Merlin born in *Tumbe*, predicted wonderful things in the beginning or entrance of this Angels Government.

Arthurus who commonly is called *Arthur*, the most glorious King of Great Britain, who overcame the *Barbarians*, restored peace to the Church, went away conqueror in many battles: propagated the Faith of Christ, subdued to his dominion all *Gallia, Norway, Denmark,* and many other Provinces. He was the most glorious of all Kings that lived in his time, who after many famous actions performed, never more appearred, being expected to return by the Britains for many years, of whom in times past many praise-worthy songs were published by the Bards of that people of wonderful Poets; for whilest he reigned, *England* was in its most flourishing condition, unto whom thirteen kingdoms were subject.

In or near these times the several Orders of *Monks* began to multiply in the Church of God: *Theodoric* King of *Gothes* being an Arian possessed all *Italy*, and murdered *Boetius* their Consul.

All manner of Estates were full of perturbation, as well as the Empire as Church affairs, or Church and Common-wealth were now in great distress.

Zenon and *Anastasius, Arrian* Emperors in the East, *Theodoric* and his successors in *Italy, Honorius* King of the *Vandalls* in *Affrica* excercised no small Tyranny.

Clodoucus King of *France* at length in Gallia being turned Christian, both overcame the *Gothes*, and restored peace in many places, though not in every Country and Kingdom.

In the time of *St. Benedict,* and year of Christ 500, or thereabouts, in the beginning of the government of this Angel *Zachariel* the Spirit of *Jupiter,* whose spirit's property it is, to change Empires and Kingdoms, which was done in this Revolution, histories manifoldly declared; and what himself could not perform, he ordained *Raphael* the Angel of *Mercury,* his successor, to perfect in *Charles* King of *French*-men.

Many Kingdoms came to their periods under these 350 years both of the *Gothes, Vandalls, Burgundians, Lumbards, Thuringers, Almains, Bavarians,* and very many besides.

Justinianus the Emperor first of all about these times beautified the Common-wealth very deservedly with his Laws.

Many gallant and most admirable men flourished under *Zachariel.*

Justinianus built the Temple of *St. Sophia* in *Constantinople,* consisting of 400 Towers. The Empire is divided and made Bi-partite, and ever and anon is more and more oppressed with mischiefs.
Many signs in heaven appeared about these times, as is easily collected from Histories.

Cosdroes king of the Persians took *Jerusalem,* whom *Heraclius* the Emperour afterward slew.

Mahomet the *Arabian* in these times about the year of Christ 600 introduced the Sect of *Sarazens*, by which Sect the Roman Empire in *Asia* is now quite extinguished.

Dagobert King of *France* slew the English, at that time called *Saxons* (whom in battle he overcame). Its remarkable, that by little and little Christianity about these times began to fail in *Asia* and *Affrick*, upon entrance of the Sect of the *Sarasins* therein, which now had almost poisoned the whole world.

About the years of our Lord God 774. Crosses appeared in the garments of men, and not long after the Roman Empire is divided, a translation of the *Monarchy* being made to *Charles* who was of the Frankes Nation in Germany, who preserved the Empire and Church from perishing, and fought many famous battles.

The name of *Western Galls,* or *Westphalians* in *Saxony* after his victory first had its beginning.

In the 18th place after finishing the rule of *Zachariel,* the Angel of *Jupiter, Raphael* the spirit of *Mercury* undertook the disposing of this worlds affaires, the third time, the second day of *November* in the year of the Creation of the World, 6023 in eighth month, and he swayed the scepter of the World 354 years and four months, until the years of the world 6378 and of our Lord God 1171.

In the first beginning of this revolution of *Raphael* the Angel of *Mercury,* the Monarchy of the Roman Empire (as we mentioned before) was translated to *Charles* the great.

After *Charles* his son *Lodowick* ruled 25 years, who being dead, his sons contending amongst themselves, did again extenuate the strength of the Empire.

The Normans harrowed *France: Rome* is twice scourged by the *Saracens*: under *Lodowick* the second it rained blood from Heaven in *Italy*, by the space of three whole days.

In *Saxony*, a certain village with all its buildings, and inhabitants was in a moment swept away by an horrible gaping or opening of the earth.

About the year of our Lord God 910, there were many great motions in *Italy*, and *Italy* fell from the Empire of the Franks or Franconians, and ordained proper kings for themselves of their own election; the first whereof was *Berengarius* the Duke of *Fonolivium*, after whom seven in order succeeded, near upon fifty years, until the translation of the Empire unto the *Germans*: The first Emperor that was thereof was *Otho*, from which time the Empire began to be reformed; unto whom *Otho* his son, and his Nephew *Otho* after succeeded in the Empire, under whose Government the Hungarians are converted to the Christian Faith. But the third *Otho* dying without children, instituted after his death Electors of the Empire in the year of Christianity 1002. even as they remain to this present day.

Jerusalem is again taken by the *Saracens*: many strange sights are seen in the air, in the Heavens, in the Earth and sea, and in waters: But *Otho* the third being dead, *Henry* the first by election of the Princes succeeded, reigned 20 years, who founded the Church of *Bamburg*, and dying a Virgin, together with his wife *Kunigunda* he shone gloriously in miracles; after whom *Conrade*, first Duke of the Francks is chosen, and ruled 20. years.

Godfrey Earl of *Bullen* also recovered the holy Land, and City of *Jerusalem* from the hands of the Infidels.

Before the end of this Revolution many signs and Prodigies were seen, and a little time after the Nation of the *Tartars* exceeded the bounds of their own Country, and did many mischiefs to the Empire of *Rome*.

There was Famine, Pestilence, Earthquakes in the Empire: Three suns were seen in the East, and as many Moons. In the year of our Lord God 1153. *Frederick* first called *Barbarossa* began to reign, and ruled 33 years, the beginning of whose Government was in the 336th year of *Raphael*: He did many noble exploits, and enlarged the strength of that Empire, performed sundry wars with great success, in whose ninth year the *Egians* and *Lituotrians* were converted to the Faith of Christ.

Samael the Angel of *Mars* in order, the nineteenth time came to accept the Gubernation of the universal world, it being now his third return, and this he did the third day of *March, Anno Mundi,* 6378 and he regulated *mundane* affaires 354 years and four months, until the years of the World 6732 and four months; and of our Lord God 1525, under whose predominancy many wars were all over the whole world, by which means infinite thousands of men perished, and sundry Kingdoms lost their former bounds: between *Frederick* the first Emperor and the Roman Nobility, many controversies arose, sundry great battels were fought, and many thousands of *Romans* perished.

The aforesaid *Frederick* did wholy subvert *Mediolanum: Leige* is destroyed, *Jerusalem* is again taken by the *Saracens*, the Empire of the *Tartarians* the greatest in the whole World about these times took its beginning, occasioned a very great plague in the World, nor yet do they cease.

After *Frederick, Henrie* his Son is elected Emperor. Who being dead, Schism confounds that Empire; under *Philip* and *Otho* many battles followed in the confines of *Germany, Argentine, Cullen, Liege, Wormes, Spires*, and all over the Kingdom. The sect of begging or Mendicant Friars began in these times, in the 40th year, or thereabouts of *Samael*: from whence it is most apparent, that all things are done by providence. The *Sarazens* fought many battels against the Christians in *Asia* and *Africk. Constantinople* is taken by the *Germans: Baldwin* Earl of *Flanders* is instituted Emperor. In *Almain* more then twenty thousand young men are drowned in the Sea by *Pyrats*, who seduced by a vain spirit, did give forth they would recover the holy land.

From *Spain* many shepherds or keepers of cattle united themselves together, coming to *Paris* dispoiling the clergy of their livelyhoods, the common people taking part with them, or being well pleased with it.

But when they extended their hands to take away the goods of the Layity, they were quite cut off and destroyed.

In the year of Christ 1212. *Frederick* the second is elected, he reigned 33 years, and did many acts against the Church. In the year 1238, an Eclipse and a continual Earthquake undid many thousands of men.

Frisia also by continual incursions of the sea, was almost wholly drowned, and there perished more then one hundred thousand of men and women.

The *Tartars* waste *Hungaria* and *Polonia, Armenia* the greater being first subdued, and many regions besides.

In the year of Christ 1244, a certain Jew digging in the ground at *Toledo* in *Spain,* found a book, in which it was written, In the third World Christ shall be born of the Virgin *Mary*, and shall suffer for the salvation of man, not long after the third World believing, shall be baptized.

It was the third Revolution of the Angel of *Saturn,* concerning which, what is spoken is intended: in the beginning of whose reign, Christ was born of a Virgin.

The Popes of *Rome* deposing *Frederick,* it is said the Empire was vacant 28 years, until the Election of *Rodolph* Count of *Habspurg,* constituting Kings by turns in the Intervals or vacancy. First *Henry* Count of *Schuvartzenburg* at *Thuring* by election of the Princes; then *William* Earle of *Holland, Conrade* the Son of *Frederick, Alfonsus* King of *Castile, Richard* Earl of

Cornwall, brother to the King of *England*, many evils were multiplied upon the face of the Earth.

At or near this time about the year of our Lord God 1260. the Confederacy of the *Switzers* began, a small people in number, but have increased with the time, who have slain many of their Nobility, and being a Warlike people have banished and frighted away many others of their Nobles from their proper habitations, whose Common wealth is now known to all the people of *Germany*.

In the year of Christians 1273, *Rudolphus* of *Habspurg* is constituted Emperor by Election of the Princes. He reigned 18 years, the best of men, prudent in all manner of affairs, from whom afterwards descended all the Dukes of *Austria*. The *Tartarians* invading the Lands of Christians, *Constantinpole* and *Greece*, brought infinite damage to the Christians.

The *Saracens* occupied many Cities in *Asia*, killing and destroying more than four hundred thousand Christians: *Rudolphus* being dead, *Adolph* of *Nassaw* is elected King, he governed six years, whom *Albert* the son of *Rudolph*, afterwards overcame and slew in a fight neer *Wormes* and was chosen Imperator in the year of Christ 1298. He governed ten years and was slain by his brother's son. The Order of the Knights Templars by command of Pope *Clement* the fifth is destroyed, the Isle of *Rhodes* is recovered by Christians out of the hands of the *Sarazens*, after the War and siege thereof had continued four whole years. *Albertus* being slain by his Nephew; *Henry* is constituted the eighth Emperor, being Count of *Luxenburg*, who reigned 5 years; he being dead *Lodowick* the fourth of *Bavaria* reigned 32 years, beginning in the year 1315, unto whom the Popes of *Rome* gave a Crown. *Frederick* Duke of *Austria* opposes himself against *Lodowick*, but is overcome by him.

After *Lodowick, Charles* the fourth King of *Bohemia* is constituted Emperor; who converted the Bishoprick of *Prague* into an Archbishoprick; he reigned 31 years: there were most fearful Earthquakes. This *Charles* did institute many things in favour of the Princes Electors, concerning their Customs and Tallys, which were not formerly in use. *Gunther* Count of *Schuartzenburg* styled himself King, opposed *Charles* the Emperor, but prevailed nothing at all against him.

After *Charles,* his Son *Winceslaus* governed 22 years: after whom *Jodocus* Marques of *Moravia* succeeded, *Sigismund* Cozen *German* of *Winceslaus.*

Winceslaus was disposed, *Leopald* Duke of *Austria*, 8 Earls, and more then 4000 souldiers fighting against the *Switzers,* were all slain by them.

During the government of *Winceslaus* King of *Bohemia* Emperor: the Tenets of *John Huss* had their beginning. *Winceslaus* being deposed, *Rupert* Count *Palatine* of *Rhine*, and Duke of *Bavaria* was elected, and ruled 10. years. In the year of our Lord God 1369, the Christians engaged themselves in a war against the *Sarazens*, which succeeded poorly, by reason of the *French* mens' Arrogancy: because more then one hundred thousand chrisitans died in that war; besides such as were made

Captives, amongst whom was *John* Duke of *Burgundy*, many were the wars of those times.

In the year of the World 1407 *Sigismund* is made Emperor, and governed 27 years: he endeavoured to waste and destroy the Kingdom of *Bohemia* thereby to extinguish Heresy, but it availed him little. The Kingdom of *France* is most grievously wasted and consumed by the *English* and *Burgundians: Sigismund* being departed this life, *Albert* Duke of *Austria, Sigismunds* son in Law, succeeded in the year of the Christians 1438. and only reigned two years, an admirable man and worthy of the Empire. He being deceased, *Frederick* the third Duke of *Austria*, the Son of *Ernestus,* by election of the Princes, is chosen Emperor: and reigned 56 years, a man of a Divine soul and peaceable conversation, who began to rule *Anno Dom.* 1440.

In the year of Christians 1453, *Constantinople* is taken of the *Turks* by Treachery of a certain *Genoway,* and a little after by degrees all *Greece* fell from their Christian faith. For a litle time after many Kingdoms and Provinces of the Christians were harrowed, wasted, and taken by the *Turks.* Many and most grievous wars the Christians had amongst themselves about this time, in *France, England, Saxony, Westphalia, Prusia, Flanders, Sweden,* and other places. In these times the Art of Printing was newly discovered, and invented at *Mogunce* the Metropolis of *Almain,* by a wonderful industry, and not without the special gift of the Deity.

In the year of Christ 1456, the *Turks* were overthrown in *Hungaria* by the faithful Christians, whereof many of

37

them perished. The Pilgrimage of young men to Saint *Michael was wonderful.* There were Earthquakes in the Kingdom of *Naples,* and more then fourty thousand people perished thereby.

In the year of the World 1462 *Moruntia* is taken and spoiled being the Metropolis of the *Franconians* or *Francks* in *Germany.*

Charles Duke of *Burgundy* overcame the *Franconians* in *Anno* 1465. After that in 1467 he destroyed the cities *Dinant et Liege, An.* 1473. He entered *Gelderland,* and with much valour obtained it, and in like manner all the whole Dukedome of *Loraigne.*

A Comet during all the month of *January* 1472 appeared. *Charles* Duke of *Burgundy* not long besieged the Town of *Nussicum* one whole years' space, videlecit in or about 1474. which Magnanimous Prince was afterwards slain in war in the year 1467. The *Turks* took away from the Christians about these times, many of their cities, *Nigropont* in *Euboia,* the Kingdom of *Bosnia,* Dukedome of *Speta, Achaia, Mysia,* and more Kingdoms besides these in the *East.*

Anno 1476 a convocation of fools was in *Franconia* of *Germany* neer *Niclaushausen,* full of errors.

Anno 1480 the *Turks* besieged the *Rhodians* with a powerful Army but did not prevail; departing the same year from *Rhodes,* they took the city *Hydruntum,* more then twelve thousand Christians were slain there, only 22 soldiers escaped. The next year *Mahomet* Emperor of the *Turks* died; to whom *Bajazet* his first born succeeded in the Kingdom, having reigned now at this present 27 years. In the year of Christ 1486, *Maximilian* the Son of *Frederick* was instituted King of *Romans* at *Franckford,* and saluted *Caesar* by *Julius* the Pope 1508, who instituted the Order of warfare of Saint *George* purposely against *Hereticks* and *Turks:* he brought the *Switzers* low by war, and even to this day makes war against the Rebellious *Sicambrians;* he will be fortunate against all such as break their Leagues or Covenants with him.

The King of *France* after his wonted manner, a constant persecutor of the Empire, is discovered to plot new devices against it. The Omnipotent protects those assigned to the Government of *Samael: Anno* 1508. the *Venetians* Rebels to the Empire of *Caesar,* are threatened with War and Banishment. Punishment of stubbornness will be the reward of an advised satisfaction. About the end of this third Revolution of *Samael,* the Image of alteration shall pass to the first and shall be the Perdition of many men for unless *Aries* be reduced again, (God assisting) (ad algos) there will be a translation of one Monarchy, or of some great Kingdom.

A strong sect of Religion shall arise, and be the overthrowing of the Ancient Religion.

It's to be feared, lest the fourth beast lose one head.

Mars first of all in the Government of *Samael* foretold the Flood, in his second return, the siege and destruction of Troy: in his third toward the end thereof will be found great want of unity: from matters

39

preceding may be Judged what will or ought to succeed. This third Revolution of *Mars* shall not be consummated without Prophecy, and the institution of some new Religion, from this year of our Lord 1508. Here yet remains until the end of the Government of *Samael* 17 years wherein signs and figures shall be given, foreshowing the beginnings of evil. For in *Anno.* 1525, crosses were seen in the garments of men by the space of ten years before, what is past already shall shew their effects: but 13 years from hence being justly summoned away, you shall surrender your place to the (*non Intelligent*) you shall revive again far greater to me, after the *Fates* in the third; unless it is lawful that you obscure yourself in a cloud.

The twentieth time in order, *Gabriel* Angel of the Moon received the moderation of the World, in the year of the World 6732, in the fourth month, and fourth day of *June:* in the year of Christ 1525, and he shall regulate the world 354. years, and four months, until the year of the world 7086 and the eighth month, but of our Lord Christ 1879 and the 11th month.

THE FUTURE SERIES OF THIS REVOLUTION REQUIRES PROPHECY.

Most sacred *Caesar,* I have not written these things assertively, nor must we believe it by any means whatever with the injury of Orthodox Divinity.

There are some that, in these things, have supputed Lunar months, which if you hold fit to consent unto, then those things I have written must be varied.

I protest with my own proper hand, and confess with my own mouth, that in all these things delivered, I believe nothing, nor admit to anything, except what the Catholic Church holds: the rest, I refute and contemn as vain, feigned and superstitious.

FINIS

Joh. Trit.

www.ingramcontent.com/pod-product-compliance
Lightning Source LLC
Chambersburg PA
CBHW070036110426
42741CB00035B/2791